TEACHERS

BY EMMA LESS

I0895035

AMICUS READERS • AMICUS INK

Amicus Readers and Amicus Ink are imprints of Amicus
P.O. Box 1329, Mankato, MN 56002
www.amicuspublishing.us

Cataloging-in-Publication Data is on file with the publisher.
ISBN 978-1-68151-299-0 (library binding)
ISBN 978-1-68152-281-4 (paperback)
ISBN 978-1-68151-361-4 (eBook)

Editor: Valerie Bodden
Designer: Patty Kelley

Photo Credits:
Cover: Iofoto/Dreamstime.com
Inside: Adobe Stock: Wavebreakmicro 3. Dreamstime.com: Monkey Business Images 6, Iofoto 8, Goldenkb 10, Photographerlondon 12, Farakos 16TL, Martinlisner 16R, Diane Miller 16B. Shutterstock: Monkey Business Images 4, 15.

Printed in China.

HC 10 9 8 7 6 5 4 3 2 1
PB 10 9 8 7 6 5 4 3 2 1

It is the first day of school.
The kids meet their teacher!

Hundreds Board

They all sit on the rug. The teacher sits between Silas and Maria.

The teacher reads
the kids a book.
He uses
funny voices.

The kids work
on letters.
The teacher helps
Katie spell Mom.

2
+ 5
5
+ 3

4+3=7

Now it is time
for math.
The teacher shows
Marla how to add.

The class
makes music.
Jake and Mia
play along.

Time to go home!
We learned
a lot today!

SEEN IN A CLASSROOM

school desk

class pet

pencils